THIS JOURNAL BELONGS TO:

_ _ _ _ _ _ _ _ _ _ _ _

ONE
Question
A DAY

A Five-Year Journal

CASTLE POINT BOOKS
NEW YORK

January 1

What goal would you like to
accomplish this year?

Year: _____ _____

_____

_____

Year: _____ _____

_____

_____

Year: _____ _____

_____

_____

Year: _____ _____

_____

_____

Year: _____ _____

_____

_____

January 2

Whom do you envy most?

Year: _____ _____

_____

_____

_____

Year: _____ _____

_____

_____

_____

Year: _____ _____

_____

_____

_____

Year: _____ _____

_____

_____

_____

Year: _____ _____

_____

_____

_____

January 3

What is one thing you learned today?

Year: _____

Year: _____

Year: _____

Year: _____

Year: _____

January 4

What is one thing you wish you
had done differently today?

Year: _____ _____

_____

_____

_____

Year: _____ _____

_____

_____

_____

Year: _____ _____

_____

_____

_____

Year: _____ _____

_____

_____

_____

Year: _____ _____

_____

_____

_____

January 5

What event or milestone are
you looking forward to?

Year: _____ _____

_____

_____

Year: _____ _____

_____

_____

Year: _____ _____

_____

_____

Year: _____ _____

_____

_____

Year: _____ _____

_____

_____

January 6

If you were an animal, what
animal would you be?

Year: _____ _____

_____

_____

Year: _____ _____

_____

_____

Year: _____ _____

_____

_____

Year: _____ _____

_____

_____

Year: _____ _____

_____

_____

January 7

What is the best news you've received lately?

Year: _____ _____
_____
_____

Year: _____ _____
_____
_____

Year: _____ _____
_____
_____

Year: _____ _____
_____
_____

Year: _____ _____
_____
_____

January 8

What age do you feel?

Year: _____ _____
_____
_____
_____

Year: _____ _____
_____
_____
_____

Year: _____ _____
_____
_____
_____

Year: _____ _____
_____
_____
_____

Year: _____ _____
_____
_____
_____

January 9

What change do you want to make?

Year: _____ _____

_____

_____

Year: _____ _____

_____

_____

Year: _____ _____

_____

_____

Year: _____ _____

_____

_____

Year: _____ _____

_____

_____

January 10

What is the last dream you remember?

Year: _____ _____

_____

_____

Year: _____ _____

_____

_____

_____

Year: _____ _____

_____

_____

Year: _____ _____

_____

_____

Year: _____ _____

_____

_____

January 11

Rate your happiness today on
a scale from 1 to 10.

Year: _____ _____

_____

_____

Year: _____ _____

_____

_____

Year: _____ _____

_____

_____

Year: _____ _____

_____

_____

Year: _____ _____

_____

_____

January 12

What famous person would you like to meet?

Year: _____ _____

_____

_____

_____

Year: _____ _____

_____

_____

_____

Year: _____ _____

_____

_____

_____

Year: _____ _____

_____

_____

_____

Year: _____ _____

_____

_____

_____

January 13

Who in your life is most like you?

Year: _____ _____

_____

_____

_____

Year: _____ _____

_____

_____

_____

Year: _____ _____

_____

_____

_____

Year: _____ _____

_____

_____

_____

Year: _____ _____

_____

_____

_____

January 14

What color best describes
your mood today?

Year: _____ _____

_____

_____

Year: _____ _____

_____

_____

Year: _____ _____

_____

_____

Year: _____ _____

_____

_____

Year: _____ _____

_____

_____

January 15

Who is the first person you thought about today?

Year: _____ _____

_____

_____

Year: _____ _____

_____

_____

Year: _____ _____

_____

_____

Year: _____ _____

_____

_____

Year: _____ _____

_____

_____

January 16

Who was especially kind to you today?

Year: _____ _____

_____

_____

Year: _____ _____

_____

_____

Year: _____ _____

_____

_____

Year: _____ _____

_____

_____

Year: _____ _____

_____

_____

January 17

What job would you like to trade your job for this week?

Year: _____

_____

_____

_____

Year: _____

_____

_____

_____

Year: _____

_____

_____

_____

Year: _____

_____

_____

_____

Year: _____

_____

_____

_____

January 18

What lie have you told recently?

Year: _____ _____

_____

_____

_____

Year: _____ _____

_____

_____

_____

Year: _____ _____

_____

_____

_____

Year: _____ _____

_____

_____

_____

Year: _____ _____

_____

_____

_____

January 19

What are you beginning to doubt?

Year: _____ _____

_____

_____

Year: _____ _____

_____

_____

Year: _____ _____

_____

_____

Year: _____ _____

_____

_____

Year: _____ _____

_____

_____

January 20

What is one thing you have
learned about life?

Year: _____ _____

_____

_____

Year: _____ _____

_____

_____

Year: _____ _____

_____

_____

Year: _____ _____

_____

_____

Year: _____ _____

_____

_____

January 21

How hard did you work today?

Year: _____ _____

_____

_____

_____

Year: _____ _____

_____

_____

_____

Year: _____ _____

_____

_____

_____

Year: _____ _____

_____

_____

_____

Year: _____ _____

_____

_____

_____

January 22

What is your favorite joke to tell?

Year: _____

_____

_____

_____

Year: _____

_____

_____

_____

Year: _____

_____

_____

_____

Year: _____

_____

_____

_____

Year: _____

_____

_____

_____

January 23

What is one thing in nature that moves you?

Year: _____

_____

_____

_____

Year: _____

_____

_____

_____

Year: _____

_____

_____

_____

Year: _____

_____

_____

_____

Year: _____

_____

_____

_____

January 24

What foods make you happiest?

Year: _____ _____
_____
_____
_____

Year: _____ _____
_____
_____
_____

Year: _____ _____
_____
_____
_____

Year: _____ _____
_____
_____
_____

Year: _____ _____
_____
_____
_____

January 25

Which room in your home is your favorite?

Year: _____

_____
_____
_____

Year: _____

_____
_____
_____

Year: _____

_____
_____
_____

Year: _____

_____
_____
_____

Year: _____

_____
_____
_____

January 26

What treasured object would you rescue from a fire?

Year: _____ _____

_____

_____

_____

Year: _____ _____

_____

_____

_____

Year: _____ _____

_____

_____

_____

Year: _____ _____

_____

_____

_____

Year: _____ _____

_____

_____

_____

January 27

What country would you like to visit some day?

Year: _____ _____

_____

_____

_____

Year: _____ _____

_____

_____

_____

Year: _____ _____

_____

_____

_____

Year: _____ _____

_____

_____

_____

Year: _____ _____

_____

_____

_____

January 28

Who are the people in your life
who really understand you?

Year: _____ _____

_____

_____

_____

Year: _____ _____

_____

_____

_____

Year: _____ _____

_____

_____

_____

Year: _____ _____

_____

_____

_____

Year: _____ _____

_____

_____

_____

January 29

What could you never give up?

Year: _____ _____

_____

_____

_____

Year: _____ _____

_____

_____

_____

Year: _____ _____

_____

_____

_____

Year: _____ _____

_____

_____

_____

Year: _____ _____

_____

_____

_____

January 30

What song could you listen
to over and over again?

Year: _____ _____

_____

_____

Year: _____ _____

_____

_____

Year: _____ _____

_____

_____

Year: _____ _____

_____

_____

Year: _____ _____

_____

_____

January 31

Who are you worried about?

Year: _____

_____

_____

_____

Year: _____

_____

_____

_____

Year: _____

_____

_____

_____

Year: _____

_____

_____

_____

Year: _____

_____

_____

_____

February 1

What is one mistake you don't regret making?

Year: _____ _____

_____

_____

Year: _____ _____

_____

_____

Year: _____ _____

_____

_____

Year: _____ _____

_____

_____

Year: _____ _____

_____

_____

February 2

What is the most you would
pay for a haircut?

Year: _____ _____

_____

_____

Year: _____ _____

_____

_____

Year: _____ _____

_____

_____

Year: _____ _____

_____

_____

Year: _____ _____

_____

_____

February 3

What is the best part of your day?

Year: _____ _____

_____

_____

Year: _____ _____

_____

_____

Year: _____ _____

_____

_____

Year: _____ _____

_____

_____

Year: _____ _____

_____

_____

February 4

What relationship in your life do
you wish you could improve?

Year: _____ _____

_____

_____

_____

Year: _____ _____

_____

_____

_____

Year: _____ _____

_____

_____

_____

Year: _____ _____

_____

_____

_____

Year: _____ _____

_____

_____

_____

February 5

What memory makes you smile?

Year: _____ _____

_____

_____

_____

Year: _____ _____

_____

_____

_____

Year: _____ _____

_____

_____

_____

Year: _____ _____

_____

_____

_____

Year: _____ _____

_____

_____

_____

February 6

What is your favorite restaurant?

Year: _____

_____
_____
_____

Year: _____

_____
_____
_____

Year: _____

_____
_____
_____

Year: _____

_____
_____
_____

Year: _____

_____
_____
_____

February 7

What person in your life is your polar opposite?

Year: _____ _____

_____

_____

_____

Year: _____ _____

_____

_____

_____

Year: _____ _____

_____

_____

_____

Year: _____ _____

_____

_____

_____

Year: _____ _____

_____

_____

_____

February 8

What is one thing you believe to be true about love?

Year: _____

_____

_____

_____

Year: _____

_____

_____

_____

Year: _____

_____

_____

_____

Year: _____

_____

_____

_____

Year: _____

_____

_____

_____

February 9

If you could rename yourself,
what name would you choose?

Year: _____

_____

_____

_____

Year: _____

_____

_____

_____

Year: _____

_____

_____

_____

Year: _____

_____

_____

_____

Year: _____

_____

_____

_____

February 10

If you could live during any time period,
which would you choose?

Year: _____ _____

_____

_____

Year: _____ _____

_____

_____

Year: _____ _____

_____

_____

Year: _____ _____

_____

_____

Year: _____ _____

_____

_____

February 11

Who is the strongest person you know?

Year: _____ _____

_____

_____

Year: _____ _____

_____

_____

Year: _____ _____

_____

_____

Year: _____ _____

_____

_____

Year: _____ _____

_____

_____

February 12

What food are you craving right now?

Year: _____ _____

_____

_____

Year: _____ _____

_____

_____

Year: _____ _____

_____

_____

Year: _____ _____

_____

_____

Year: _____ _____

_____

_____

February 13

If you won a million dollars,
what would you buy first?

Year: _____ _____

_____

_____

_____

Year: _____ _____

_____

_____

_____

Year: _____ _____

_____

_____

_____

Year: _____ _____

_____

_____

_____

Year: _____ _____

_____

_____

_____

February 14

Who is your valentine?

Year: _____ _____

_____

_____

Year: _____ _____

_____

_____

Year: _____ _____

_____

_____

Year: _____ _____

_____

_____

Year: _____ _____

_____

_____

February 15

With whom did you have a
meaningful conversation today?

Year: _____

_____
_____
_____

Year: _____

_____
_____
_____

Year: _____

_____
_____
_____

Year: _____

_____
_____
_____

Year: _____

_____
_____
_____

February 16

What are you shy about?

Year: _____ _____

_____

_____

_____

Year: _____ _____

_____

_____

_____

Year: _____ _____

_____

_____

_____

Year: _____ _____

_____

_____

_____

Year: _____ _____

_____

_____

_____

February 17

Which holiday do you most
look forward to?

Year: _____ _____

_____

_____

Year: _____ _____

_____

_____

Year: _____ _____

_____

_____

Year: _____ _____

_____

_____

Year: _____ _____

_____

_____

February 18

Who could have been nicer to you today?

Year: _____ _____

_____

_____

Year: _____ _____

_____

_____

Year: _____ _____

_____

_____

Year: _____ _____

_____

_____

Year: _____ _____

_____

_____

February 19

When was the last time you
were really angry?

Year: _____ _____

_____

_____

Year: _____ _____

_____

_____

Year: _____ _____

_____

_____

Year: _____ _____

_____

_____

Year: _____ _____

_____

_____

February 20

On what do you spend way too much money?

Year: _____ _____

_____

_____

_____

Year: _____ _____

_____

_____

_____

Year: _____ _____

_____

_____

_____

Year: _____ _____

_____

_____

_____

Year: _____ _____

_____

_____

_____

February 21

When was the last time you cried?

Year: _____ _____

_____

_____

Year: _____ _____

_____

_____

Year: _____ _____

_____

_____

Year: _____ _____

_____

_____

Year: _____ _____

_____

_____

February 22

What do you see outside of your window?

Year: _____

_____

_____

_____

Year: _____

_____

_____

_____

Year: _____

_____

_____

_____

Year: _____

_____

_____

_____

Year: _____

_____

_____

_____

February 23

What struggle are you happy
to have behind you?

Year: _____ _____

_____

_____

_____

Year: _____ _____

_____

_____

_____

Year: _____ _____

_____

_____

_____

Year: _____ _____

_____

_____

_____

Year: _____ _____

_____

_____

_____

February 24

What promise have you kept?

Year: _____ _____

_____

_____

Year: _____ _____

_____

_____

Year: _____ _____

_____

_____

Year: _____ _____

_____

_____

Year: _____ _____

_____

_____

February 25

What is the first thing you did this morning?

Year: _____ _____

_____

_____

_____

Year: _____ _____

_____

_____

_____

Year: _____ _____

_____

_____

_____

Year: _____ _____

_____

_____

_____

Year: _____ _____

_____

_____

_____

February 26

How famous would you like to be?

Year: _____ _____

_____

_____

Year: _____ _____

_____

_____

Year: _____ _____

_____

_____

Year: _____ _____

_____

_____

Year: _____ _____

_____

_____

February 27

What are the top qualities of your perfect mate?

Year: _____

_____

_____

_____

Year: _____

_____

_____

_____

Year: _____

_____

_____

_____

Year: _____

_____

_____

_____

Year: _____

_____

_____

_____

February 28

When life gives you lemons,
what do you do?

Year: _____

_____

_____

_____

Year: _____

_____

_____

_____

Year: _____

_____

_____

_____

Year: _____

_____

_____

_____

Year: _____

_____

_____

_____

February 29
(Leap Day)

When have you taken a leap of faith?

Year: _____ _____

_____

_____

Year: _____ _____

_____

_____

Year: _____ _____

_____

_____

Year: _____ _____

_____

_____

Year: _____ _____

_____

_____

March 1

Who makes you feel appreciated?

Year: _____ _____

_____

_____

Year: _____ _____

_____

_____

Year: _____ _____

_____

_____

Year: _____ _____

_____

_____

Year: _____ _____

_____

_____

March 2

What is your favorite day of the week?

Year: _____ _____

_____

_____

_____

Year: _____ _____

_____

_____

_____

Year: _____ _____

_____

_____

_____

Year: _____ _____

_____

_____

_____

Year: _____ _____

_____

_____

_____

March 3

What about your life is different
than you expected it to be?

Year: _____ _____

_____

_____

Year: _____ _____

_____

_____

Year: _____ _____

_____

_____

Year: _____ _____

_____

_____

Year: _____ _____

_____

_____

March 4

Who was the last person you
talked to on the phone?

Year: _____ _____

_____

_____

Year: _____ _____

_____

_____

Year: _____ _____

_____

_____

Year: _____ _____

_____

_____

Year: _____ _____

_____

_____

March 5

What are you most proud of?

Year: _____ _____

_____

_____

Year: _____ _____

_____

_____

Year: _____ _____

_____

_____

Year: _____ _____

_____

_____

Year: _____ _____

_____

_____

March 6

What outfit would you wear
every day if you could?

Year: _____ _____

_____

_____

Year: _____ _____

_____

_____

Year: _____ _____

_____

_____

Year: _____ _____

_____

_____

Year: _____ _____

_____

_____

March 7

Do you feel blessed or cursed?

Year: _____ _____

_____

_____

Year: _____ _____

_____

_____

Year: _____ _____

_____

_____

Year: _____ _____

_____

_____

Year: _____ _____

_____

_____

March 8

What is your biggest fear?

Year: _____ _____

_____

_____

Year: _____ _____

_____

_____

Year: _____ _____

_____

_____

Year: _____ _____

_____

_____

Year: _____ _____

_____

_____

March 9

What was the last courageous
thing you did?

Year: _____ _____

_____

_____

Year: _____ _____

_____

_____

Year: _____ _____

_____

_____

Year: _____ _____

_____

_____

Year: _____ _____

_____

_____

March 10

Who always has your support?

Year: _____ _____

_____

_____

_____

Year: _____ _____

_____

_____

_____

Year: _____ _____

_____

_____

_____

Year: _____ _____

_____

_____

_____

Year: _____ _____

_____

_____

_____

March 11

What friendship has grown deeper?

Year: _____ _____

_____

_____

_____

Year: _____ _____

_____

_____

_____

Year: _____ _____

_____

_____

_____

Year: _____ _____

_____

_____

_____

Year: _____ _____

_____

_____

_____

March 12

What is the last movie you went to see?

Year: _____ _____

_____

_____

Year: _____ _____

_____

_____

Year: _____ _____

_____

_____

Year: _____ _____

_____

_____

Year: _____ _____

_____

_____

March 13

In what position do you sleep best?

Year: _____ _____

_____

_____

Year: _____ _____

_____

_____

Year: _____ _____

_____

_____

Year: _____ _____

_____

_____

Year: _____ _____

_____

_____

March 14

On which topic do you consider
yourself an expert?

Year: _____ _____

_____

_____

_____

Year: _____ _____

_____

_____

_____

Year: _____ _____

_____

_____

_____

Year: _____ _____

_____

_____

_____

Year: _____ _____

_____

_____

_____

March 15

What TV show always makes you laugh?

Year: _____ _____

_____

_____

Year: _____ _____

_____

_____

Year: _____ _____

_____

_____

Year: _____ _____

_____

_____

Year: _____ _____

_____

_____

March 16

What is your dream car?

Year: _____ _____

_____

_____

_____

Year: _____ _____

_____

_____

_____

Year: _____ _____

_____

_____

_____

Year: _____ _____

_____

_____

_____

Year: _____ _____

_____

_____

_____

March 17

What is your good luck charm?

Year: _____ _____

_____

_____

Year: _____ _____

_____

_____

Year: _____ _____

_____

_____

Year: _____ _____

_____

_____

Year: _____ _____

_____

_____

March 18

If your life had a theme song,
what would it be?

Year: _____

_____

_____

_____

Year: _____

_____

_____

_____

Year: _____

_____

_____

_____

Year: _____

_____

_____

_____

Year: _____

_____

_____

_____

March 19

Appetizers, dessert, or both?

Year: _____ _____

_____

_____

_____

Year: _____ _____

_____

_____

_____

Year: _____ _____

_____

_____

_____

Year: _____ _____

_____

_____

_____

Year: _____ _____

_____

_____

_____

March 20

What hasn't changed about
you over the years?

Year: _____ _____

_____

_____

Year: _____ _____

_____

_____

Year: _____ _____

_____

_____

Year: _____ _____

_____

_____

Year: _____ _____

_____

_____

March 21

What did you do exactly right today?

Year: _____

_____

_____

_____

Year: _____

_____

_____

_____

Year: _____

_____

_____

_____

Year: _____

_____

_____

_____

Year: _____

_____

_____

_____

March 22

What is on your bedside table right now?

Year: _____ _____

_____

_____

Year: _____ _____

_____

_____

Year: _____ _____

_____

_____

Year: _____ _____

_____

_____

Year: _____ _____

_____

_____

March 23

What makes you feel like a kid again?

Year: _____ _____

_____

_____

_____

Year: _____ _____

_____

_____

_____

Year: _____ _____

_____

_____

_____

Year: _____ _____

_____

_____

_____

Year: _____ _____

_____

_____

_____

March 24

Who is your mentor?

Year: _____ _____

_____

_____

Year: _____ _____

_____

_____

Year: _____ _____

_____

_____

Year: _____ _____

_____

_____

Year: _____ _____

_____

_____

March 25

Who owes you an apology?

Year: _____ _____

_____

_____

Year: _____ _____

_____

_____

Year: _____ _____

_____

_____

Year: _____ _____

_____

_____

Year: _____ _____

_____

_____

March 26

What is the last compliment you received?

Year: _____ _____

_____

_____

_____

Year: _____ _____

_____

_____

_____

Year: _____ _____

_____

_____

_____

Year: _____ _____

_____

_____

_____

Year: _____ _____

_____

_____

_____

March 27

Which year of your life
has been the most enjoyable?

Year: _____

Year: _____

Year: _____

Year: _____

Year: _____

March 28

How many cups of coffee did you drink today?

Year: _____ _____

_____

_____

Year: _____ _____

_____

_____

Year: _____ _____

_____

_____

Year: _____ _____

_____

_____

Year: _____ _____

_____

_____

March 29

What is your idea of a great evening out?

Year: _____ _____

_____

_____

Year: _____ _____

_____

_____

Year: _____ _____

_____

_____

Year: _____ _____

_____

_____

Year: _____ _____

_____

_____

March 30

Truth or dare?

Year: _____ _____

Year: _____ _____

Year: _____ _____

Year: _____ _____

March 31

City, suburbs, or country life:
Which suits you best?

Year: _____ _____

_____

_____

Year: _____ _____

_____

_____

Year: _____ _____

_____

_____

Year: _____ _____

_____

_____

Year: _____ _____

_____

_____

April 1

What is the last trick you fell for?

Year: _____ _____

_____

_____

Year: _____ _____

_____

_____

Year: _____ _____

_____

_____

Year: _____ _____

_____

_____

Year: _____ _____

_____

_____

April 2

What annoyed you or made
you cringe today?

Year: _____

Year: _____

Year: _____

Year: _____

Year: _____

April 3

What scent makes you happiest?

Year: _____ _____

_____

_____

Year: _____ _____

_____

_____

Year: _____ _____

_____

_____

Year: _____ _____

_____

_____

Year: _____ _____

_____

_____

April 4

What is the formula for success?

Year: _____

Year: _____

Year: _____

Year: _____

Year: _____

April 5

What is the last thing you searched for?

Year: _____ _____

_____

_____

Year: _____ _____

_____

_____

Year: _____ _____

_____

_____

Year: _____ _____

_____

_____

Year: _____ _____

_____

_____

April 6

What did you forget to do today?

Year: _____

_____

_____

_____

Year: _____

_____

_____

_____

Year: _____

_____

_____

_____

Year: _____

_____

_____

_____

Year: _____

_____

_____

_____

April 7

What surprised you today?

Year: _____ _____

_____

_____

_____

Year: _____ _____

_____

_____

_____

Year: _____ _____

_____

_____

_____

Year: _____ _____

_____

_____

_____

Year: _____ _____

_____

_____

_____

April 8

What is the quickest way to your heart?

Year: _____ _____

_____

_____

Year: _____ _____

_____

_____

Year: _____ _____

_____

_____

Year: _____ _____

_____

_____

Year: _____ _____

_____

_____

April 9

What is one thing you've never done?

Year: _____ _____

_____

_____

Year: _____ _____

_____

_____

Year: _____ _____

_____

_____

Year: _____ _____

_____

_____

Year: _____ _____

_____

_____

April 10

How soundly do you sleep?

Year: _____ _____

_____

_____

_____

Year: _____ _____

_____

_____

_____

Year: _____ _____

_____

_____

_____

Year: _____ _____

_____

_____

_____

Year: _____ _____

_____

_____

_____

April 11

Whose phone number(s) do
you know by heart?

Year: _____ _____

_____

_____

_____

Year: _____ _____

_____

_____

_____

Year: _____ _____

_____

_____

_____

Year: _____ _____

_____

_____

_____

Year: _____ _____

_____

_____

_____

April 12

Whose heart have you broken?

Year: _____ _____

_____

_____

Year: _____ _____

_____

_____

Year: _____ _____

_____

_____

Year: _____ _____

_____

_____

Year: _____ _____

_____

_____

April 13

What was the last vacation
you really enjoyed?

Year: _____ _____

_____

_____

_____

Year: _____ _____

_____

_____

_____

Year: _____ _____

_____

_____

_____

Year: _____ _____

_____

_____

_____

Year: _____ _____

_____

_____

_____

April 14

What is your mantra?

Year: _____ _____

_____

_____

Year: _____ _____

_____

_____

Year: _____ _____

_____

_____

Year: _____ _____

_____

_____

Year: _____ _____

_____

_____

April 15

What are the news headlines today?

Year: _____ _____

_____

_____

_____

Year: _____ _____

_____

_____

_____

Year: _____ _____

_____

_____

_____

Year: _____ _____

_____

_____

_____

Year: _____ _____

_____

_____

_____

April 16

How do you think people describe you?

Year: _____ _____

_____

_____

_____

Year: _____ _____

_____

_____

_____

Year: _____ _____

_____

_____

_____

Year: _____ _____

_____

_____

_____

Year: _____ _____

_____

_____

_____

April 17

What is your most attractive quality?

Year: _____ _____

_____

_____

Year: _____ _____

_____

_____

Year: _____ _____

_____

_____

Year: _____ _____

_____

_____

Year: _____ _____

_____

_____

April 18

Train, car, or airplane?

Year: _____ _____

_____

_____

Year: _____ _____

_____

_____

Year: _____ _____

_____

_____

Year: _____ _____

_____

_____

Year: _____ _____

_____

_____

April 19

What do you wish someone
would hurry up and invent?

Year: _____ _____

_____

_____

Year: _____ _____

_____

_____

Year: _____ _____

_____

_____

Year: _____ _____

_____

_____

Year: _____ _____

_____

_____

April 20

What was the last big purchase you made?

Year: _____ _____ _____

_____

_____

Year: _____ _____

_____

_____

Year: _____ _____

_____

_____

Year: _____ _____

_____

_____

Year: _____ _____

_____

_____

April 21

What is the last thing you did
before going to bed last night?

Year: _____ _____

_____

_____

Year: _____ _____

_____

_____

Year: _____ _____

_____

_____

Year: _____ _____

_____

_____

Year: _____ _____

_____

_____

April 22

Would you rather settle
in or venture out?

Year: _____ _____

_____

_____

_____

Year: _____ _____

_____

_____

_____

Year: _____ _____

_____

_____

_____

Year: _____ _____

_____

_____

_____

Year: _____ _____

_____

_____

_____

April 23

What problem are you having
trouble solving?

Year: _____ _____

_____

_____

Year: _____ _____

_____

_____

Year: _____ _____

_____

_____

Year: _____ _____

_____

_____

Year: _____ _____

_____

_____

April 24

What habit are you trying to break?

Year: _____ _____

_____

_____

Year: _____ _____

_____

_____

Year: _____ _____

_____

_____

Year: _____ _____

_____

_____

Year: _____ _____

_____

_____

April 25

Who is your best friend?

Year: _____ _____

_____

_____

_____

Year: _____ _____

_____

_____

_____

Year: _____ _____

_____

_____

_____

Year: _____ _____

_____

_____

_____

Year: _____ _____

_____

_____

_____

April 26

Are you a saver or a spender?

Year: _____ _____

_____

_____

_____

Year: _____ _____

_____

_____

_____

Year: _____ _____

_____

_____

_____

Year: _____ _____

_____

_____

_____

Year: _____ _____

_____

_____

_____

April 27

Is technology your friend or your foe?

Year: _____ _____
_____
_____

Year: _____ _____
_____
_____

Year: _____ _____
_____
_____

Year: _____ _____
_____
_____

Year: _____ _____
_____
_____

April 28

What movie do you rave about?

Year: _____ _____

_____

_____

Year: _____ _____

_____

_____

Year: _____ _____

_____

_____

Year: _____ _____

_____

_____

Year: _____ _____

_____

_____

April 29

What food do you cook the most?

Year: _____ _____

_____

_____

Year: _____ _____

_____

_____

Year: _____ _____

_____

_____

Year: _____ _____

_____

_____

Year: _____ _____

_____

_____

April 30

What comforts you in the worst of times?

Year: _____ _____

_____

_____

Year: _____ _____

_____

_____

Year: _____ _____

_____

_____

Year: _____ _____

_____

_____

Year: _____ _____

_____

_____

May 1

What household chore do you avoid?

Year: _____ _____

_____

_____

Year: _____ _____

_____

_____

Year: _____ _____

_____

_____

Year: _____ _____

_____

_____

Year: _____ _____

_____

_____

May 2

What natural talents do you have?

Year: _____ _____

_____

_____

_____

Year: _____ _____

_____

_____

_____

Year: _____ _____

_____

_____

_____

Year: _____ _____

_____

_____

_____

Year: _____ _____

_____

_____

_____

May 3

What are you saving your money for?

Year: _____ _____

_____

_____

Year: _____ _____

_____

_____

Year: _____ _____

_____

_____

Year: _____ _____

_____

_____

Year: _____ _____

_____

_____

May 4

What question would you
most like answered?

Year: _____ _____

_____

_____

Year: _____ _____

_____

_____

_____

Year: _____ _____

_____

_____

Year: ___ ___ _____

_____

_____

Year: _____ _____

_____

_____

May 5

If tomorrow were your last day on
Earth, how would you spend it?

Year: _____ _____

_____

_____

_____

Year: _____ _____

_____

_____

_____

Year: _____ _____

_____

_____

_____

Year: _____ _____

_____

_____

_____

Year: _____ _____

_____

_____

_____

May 6

What do you think will be different
in your life next year?

Year: _____ _____

_____

_____

Year: _____ _____

_____

_____

Year: _____ _____

_____

_____

Year: _____ _____

_____

_____

Year: _____ _____

_____

_____

May 7

Have you ever witnessed something miraculous?

Year: _____ _____

_____

_____

Year: _____ _____

_____

_____

Year: _____ _____

_____

_____

Year: _____ _____

_____

_____

Year: _____ _____

_____

_____

May 8

What gets better as you get older?

Year: _____ _____

_____

_____

Year: _____ _____

_____

_____

_____

Year: _____ _____

_____

_____

_____

Year: _____ _____

_____

_____

_____

Year: _____ _____

_____

_____

_____

May 9

Who or what do you enjoy taking care of?

Year: _____ _____

_____

_____

Year: _____ _____

_____

_____

Year: _____ _____

_____

_____

Year: _____ _____

_____

_____

Year: _____ _____

_____

_____

May 10

Who inspires you?

Year: _____

_____

_____

_____

Year: _____

_____

_____

_____

Year: _____

_____

_____

_____

Year: _____

_____

_____

_____

Year: _____

_____

_____

_____

May 11

Whom do you most want to impress?

Year: _____ _____

_____

_____

Year: _____ _____

_____

_____

Year: _____ _____

_____

_____

Year: _____ _____

_____

_____

Year: _____ _____

_____

_____

May 12

How well did you treat yourself today?

Year: _____ _____

_____

_____

Year: _____ _____

_____

_____

Year: _____ _____

_____

_____

Year: _____ _____

_____

_____

Year: _____ _____

_____

_____

May 13

When was the last time you threw a party?

Year: _____ _____

_____

_____

Year: _____ _____

_____

_____

Year: _____ _____

_____

_____

Year: _____ _____

_____

_____

Year: _____ _____

_____

_____

May 14

What is your favorite kind of weather?

Year: _____ _____

_____

_____

_____

Year: _____ _____

_____

_____

_____

Year: _____ _____

_____

_____

_____

Year: _____ _____

_____

_____

_____

Year: _____ _____

_____

_____

_____

May 15

What time did you go to bed last night?

Year: _____ _____

_____

_____

Year: _____ _____

_____

_____

Year: _____ _____

_____

_____

Year: _____ _____

_____

_____

Year: _____ _____

_____

_____

May 16

Who challenges you?

Year: _____

_____

_____

_____

Year: _____

_____

_____

_____

Year: _____

_____

_____

_____

Year: _____

_____

_____

_____

Year: _____

_____

_____

_____

May 17

What was the last photo you took?

Year: _____ _____

_____

_____

_____

Year: _____ _____

_____

_____

_____

Year: _____ _____

_____

_____

_____

Year: _____ _____

_____

_____

_____

Year: _____ _____

_____

_____

_____

May 18

Are you usually early,
on time, or late for events?

Year: _____ _____

_____

_____

_____

Year: _____ _____

_____

_____

_____

Year: _____ _____

_____

_____

_____

Year: _____ _____

_____

_____

_____

Year: _____ _____

_____

_____

_____

May 19

What is on your to-do list this week?

Year: _____ _____

_____

_____

Year: _____ _____

_____

_____

Year: _____ _____

_____

_____

Year: _____ _____

_____

_____

Year: _____ _____

_____

_____

May 20

What was the last website you visited?

Year: _____ _____

_____

_____

_____

Year: _____ _____

_____

_____

_____

Year: _____ _____

_____

_____

_____

Year: _____ _____

_____

_____

_____

Year: _____ _____

_____

_____

_____

May 21

If your life were a book, what
would be the title?

Year: _____ _____

_____

_____

_____

Year: _____ _____

_____

_____

_____

Year: _____ _____

_____

_____

_____

Year: _____ _____

_____

_____

_____

Year: _____ _____

_____

_____

_____

May 22

What is unique about this chapter of your life?

Year: _____ _____

_____

_____

Year: _____ _____

_____

_____

Year: _____ _____

_____

_____

Year: _____ _____

_____

_____

Year: _____ _____

_____

_____

May 23

What do you wish you had
done better today?

Year: _____ _____

_____

_____

_____

Year: _____ _____

_____

_____

_____

Year: _____ _____

_____

_____

_____

Year: _____ _____

_____

_____

_____

Year: _____ _____

_____

_____

_____

May 24

What is the messiest room
or area of your home?

Year: _____ _____

_____

_____

_____

Year: _____ _____

_____

_____

_____

Year: _____ _____

_____

_____

_____

Year: _____ _____

_____

_____

_____

Year: _____ _____

_____

_____

_____

May 25

What was the last thing you
forced yourself to do?

Year: _____

_____

Year: _____

_____

Year: _____

_____

Year: _____

_____

Year: _____

_____

May 26

What do you miss most
about being younger?

Year: _____ _____

_____

_____

_____

Year: _____ _____

_____

_____

_____

Year: _____ _____

_____

_____

_____

Year: _____ _____

_____

_____

_____

Year: _____ _____

_____

_____

_____

May 27

What memory do you wish you
could erase or rewrite?

Year: _____ _____

_____

_____

Year: _____ _____

_____

_____

Year: _____ _____

_____

_____

Year: _____ _____

_____

_____

Year: _____ _____

_____

_____

May 28

What do you look forward to
about growing older?

Year: _____

_____

_____

_____

Year: _____

_____

_____

_____

Year: _____

_____

_____

_____

Year: _____

_____

_____

_____

Year: _____

_____

_____

_____

May 29

What term of endearment
do you use most?

Year: _____ _____

_____

_____

Year: _____ _____

_____

_____

Year: _____ _____

_____

_____

Year: _____ _____

_____

_____

Year: _____ _____

_____

_____

May 30

Are you working in the right job?

Year: _____

_____

_____

_____

Year: _____

_____

_____

_____

Year: _____

_____

_____

_____

Year: _____

_____

_____

_____

Year: _____

_____

_____

_____

May 31

What did you want to say
today that you didn't?

Year: _____ _____

_____

_____

Year: _____ _____

_____

_____

Year: _____ _____

_____

_____

Year: _____ _____

_____

_____

Year: _____ _____

_____

_____

June 1

What made you smile today?

Year: _____ _____

_____

_____

_____

Year: _____ _____

_____

_____

_____

Year: _____ _____

_____

_____

_____

Year: _____ _____

_____

_____

_____

Year: _____ _____

_____

_____

_____

June 2

If you could read the future, would you?

Year: _____ _____

_____

_____

Year: _____ _____

_____

_____

Year: _____ _____

_____

_____

Year: _____ _____

_____

_____

Year: _____ _____

_____

_____

June 3

Who is the star of your family?

Year: _____ _____

_____

_____

Year: _____ _____

_____

_____

Year: _____ _____

_____

_____

Year: _____ _____

_____

_____

Year: _____ _____

_____

_____

June 4

Who was the last person to
knock on your door?

Year: _____ _____

_____

_____

Year: _____ _____

_____

_____

Year: _____ _____

_____

_____

Year: _____ _____

_____

_____

Year: _____ _____

_____

_____

June 5

Whom do you most want to
hang out with today?

Year: _____ _____

_____

_____

Year: _____ _____

_____

_____

Year: _____ _____

_____

_____

Year: _____ _____

_____

_____

Year: _____ _____

_____

_____

June 6

What superstitions do you have?

Year: _____ _____

_____

_____

Year: _____ _____

_____

_____

Year: _____ _____

_____

_____

Year: _____ _____

_____

_____

Year: _____ _____

_____

_____

June 7

What nickname do you like for yourself?

Year: _____

_____

_____

_____

Year: _____

_____

_____

_____

Year: _____

_____

_____

_____

Year: _____

_____

_____

_____

Year: _____

_____

_____

_____

June 8

I never want to be far from _____.

Year: _____   _____

_____

_____

_____

Year: _____   _____

_____

_____

_____

Year: _____   _____

_____

_____

_____

Year: _____   _____

_____

_____

_____

Year: _____   _____

_____

_____

_____

June 9

What big decision have
you made recently?

Year: _____ _____

_____

_____

Year: _____ _____

_____

_____

Year: _____ _____

_____

_____

Year: _____ _____

_____

_____

Year: _____ _____

_____

_____

June 10

My life felt like it hadn't begun
until _____.

Year: _____ _____

_____

_____

_____

Year: _____ _____

_____

_____

_____

Year: _____ _____

_____

_____

_____

Year: _____ _____

_____

_____

_____

Year: _____ _____

_____

_____

_____

June 11

Fate or free will?

Year: _____ _____

_____

_____

Year: _____ _____

_____

_____

Year: _____ _____

_____

_____

Year: _____ _____

_____

_____

Year: _____ _____

_____

_____

June 12

From what are you trying to escape?

Year: _____ _____

_____

_____

_____

Year: _____ _____

_____

_____

_____

Year: _____ _____

_____

_____

_____

Year: _____ _____

_____

_____

_____

Year: _____ _____

_____

_____

_____

June 13

Which best describes your lifestyle:
sneakers, dress shoes, or sandals?

Year: _____ _____

_____

_____

Year: _____ _____

_____

_____

Year: _____ _____

_____

_____

Year: _____ _____

_____

_____

Year: _____ _____

_____

_____

June 14

What is the last gift you gave to someone?

Year: _____ _____

_____

_____

_____

Year: _____ _____

_____

_____

_____

Year: _____ _____

_____

_____

_____

Year: _____ _____

_____

_____

_____

Year: _____ _____

_____

_____

_____

June 15

What puts you to sleep?

Year: _____ ___ _____

_____

_____

_____

Year: _____ ___ _____

_____

_____

_____

Year: _____ ___ _____

_____

_____

_____

Year: _____ ___ _____

_____

_____

_____

Year: _____ ___ _____

_____

_____

_____

June 16

What foreign language sounds best to your ears?

Year: _____ _____

_____

_____

Year: _____ _____

_____

_____

Year: _____ _____

_____

_____

Year: _____ _____

_____

_____

Year: _____ _____

_____

_____

June 17

What worked in your favor today?

Year: _____ _____

_____

_____

Year: _____ _____

_____

_____

Year: _____ _____

_____

_____

Year: _____ _____

_____

_____

Year: _____ _____

_____

_____

June 18

Whom do you owe in a big way?

Year: _____ _____

_____

_____

Year: _____ _____

_____

_____

Year: _____ _____

_____

_____

Year: _____ _____

_____

_____

Year: _____ _____

_____

_____

June 19

Whom or what do you wish
you cared about more?

Year: _____ _____

_____

_____

_____

Year: _____ _____

_____

_____

_____

Year: _____ _____

_____

_____

_____

Year: _____ _____

_____

_____

_____

Year: _____ _____

_____

_____

_____

June 20

What are you looking forward to?

Year: _____ _____

_____

_____

Year: _____ _____

_____

_____

Year: _____ _____

_____

_____

Year: _____ _____

_____

_____

Year: _____ _____

_____

_____

June 21

What did you avoid doing today?

Year: _____ _____

_____

_____

_____

Year: _____ _____

_____

_____

_____

Year: _____ _____

_____

_____

_____

Year: _____ _____

_____

_____

_____

Year: _____ _____

_____

_____

_____

June 22

Something I need more of in
my life is _____.

Year: _____   _____

_____

_____

_____

Year: _____   _____

_____

_____

_____

Year: _____   _____

_____

_____

_____

Year: _____   _____

_____

_____

_____

Year: _____   _____

_____

_____

_____

June 23

Homemade food today or takeout?

Year: _____ _____

_____

_____

Year: _____ _____

_____

_____

Year: _____ _____

_____

_____

Year: _____ _____

_____

_____

Year: _____ _____

_____

_____

June 24

What favor did you do for
someone recently?

Year: _____ _____

_____

_____

Year: _____ _____

_____

_____

Year: _____ _____

_____

_____

Year: _____ _____

_____

_____

Year: _____ _____

_____

_____

June 25

How much time did you spend outside today?

Year: _____ _____

_____

_____

_____

Year: _____ _____

_____

_____

_____

Year: _____ _____

_____

_____

_____

Year: _____ _____

_____

_____

_____

Year: _____ _____

_____

_____

_____

June 26

What wallpaper do you have on
your phone or computer screen?

Year: _____ _____

_____

_____

_____

Year: _____ _____

_____

_____

_____

Year: _____ _____

_____

_____

_____

Year: _____ _____

_____

_____

_____

Year: _____ _____

_____

_____

_____

June 27

One person I can't figure
out is _____.

Year: _____ _____

_____

_____

Year: _____ _____

_____

_____

Year: _____ _____

_____

_____

Year: _____ _____

_____

_____

Year: _____ _____

_____

_____

June 28

Whose respect have you earned?

Year: _____ _____

_____

_____

Year: _____ _____

_____

_____

Year: _____ _____

_____

_____

Year: _____ _____

_____

_____

Year: _____ _____

_____

_____

June 29

Who makes you a better person?

Year: _____ _____

_____

_____

Year: _____ _____

_____

_____

Year: _____ _____

_____

_____

Year: _____ _____

_____

_____

Year: _____ _____

_____

_____

June 30

What rituals make you happy?

Year: _____ _____
_____
_____
_____

Year: _____ _____
_____
_____
_____

Year: _____ _____
_____
_____
_____

Year: _____ _____
_____
_____
_____

Year: _____ _____
_____
_____
_____

July 1

What is the biggest change in your
life since this time last year?

Year: _____ _____

_____

_____

_____

Year: _____ _____

_____

_____

_____

Year: _____ _____

_____

_____

_____

Year: _____ _____

_____

_____

_____

Year: _____ _____

_____

_____

_____

July 2

What do you do when no one is watching?

Year: _____ _____

_____

_____

_____

Year: _____ _____

_____

_____

_____

Year: _____ _____

_____

_____

_____

Year: _____ _____

_____

_____

_____

Year: _____ _____

_____

_____

_____

July 3

Who is the funniest person you know?

Year: _____ _____

_____

_____

_____

Year: _____ _____

_____

_____

_____

Year: _____ _____

_____

_____

_____

Year: _____ _____

_____

_____

_____

Year: _____ _____

_____

_____

_____

July 4

What makes you feel patriotic?

Year: _____ _____

_____

_____

Year: _____ _____

_____

_____

Year: _____ _____

_____

_____

Year: _____ _____

_____

_____

Year: _____ _____

_____

_____

July 5

What made you laugh out loud today?

Year: _____ _____

_____

_____

_____

Year: _____ _____

_____

_____

_____

Year: _____ _____

_____

_____

_____

Year: _____ _____

_____

_____

_____

Year: _____ _____

_____

_____

_____

July 6

What is the last commitment you made?

Year: _____ _____

_____

_____

Year: _____ _____

_____

_____

Year: _____ _____

_____

_____

Year: _____ _____

_____

_____

Year: _____ _____

_____

_____

July 7

If you could be the world champion
of something, what would it be?

Year: _____ _____

_____

_____

Year: _____ _____

_____

_____

_____

Year: _____ _____

_____

_____

Year: _____ _____

_____

_____

_____

Year: _____ _____

_____

_____

_____

July 8

Write a newspaper headline
that describes your day.

Year: _____ _____

_____

_____

_____

Year: _____ _____

_____

_____

_____

Year: _____ _____

_____

_____

_____

Year: _____ _____

_____

_____

_____

Year: _____ _____

_____

_____

_____

July 9

The person I'm most proud to be
related to is _____.

Year: _____

_____

_____

_____

Year: _____

_____

_____

_____

Year: _____

_____

_____

_____

Year: _____

_____

_____

_____

Year: _____

_____

_____

_____

July 10

I wish I had kept in touch
with _____.

Year: _____ _____

_____

_____

_____

Year: _____ _____

_____

_____

_____

Year: _____ _____

_____

_____

_____

Year: _____ _____

_____

_____

_____

Year: _____ _____

_____

_____

_____

July 11

Whom do you keep meaning
to make plans with?

Year: _____ _____

_____

_____

_____

Year: _____ _____

_____

_____

_____

Year: _____ _____

_____

_____

_____

Year: _____ _____

_____

_____

_____

Year: _____ _____

_____

_____

_____

July 12

What plan on your social calendar
do you wish you could cancel?

Year: _____ _____

_____

_____

_____

Year: _____ _____

_____

_____

_____

Year: _____ _____

_____

_____

_____

Year: _____ _____

_____

_____

_____

Year: _____ _____

_____

_____

_____

July 13

What did you do repeatedly today?

Year: _____ _____

_____

_____

Year: _____ _____

_____

_____

Year: _____ _____

_____

_____

Year: _____ _____

_____

_____

Year: _____ _____

_____

_____

July 14

Whom did you talk to the most today?

Year: _____ _____

_____

_____

Year: _____ _____

_____

_____

Year: _____ _____

_____

_____

Year: _____ _____

_____

_____

Year: _____ _____

_____

_____

July 15

What beautiful thing did
you admire today?

Year: _____

_____

_____

_____

Year: _____

_____

_____

_____

Year: _____

_____

_____

_____

Year: _____

_____

_____

_____

Year: _____

_____

_____

_____

July 16

Home is where the _____ is.

Year: _____ _____
_____
_____
_____

Year: _____ _____
_____
_____
_____

Year: _____ _____
_____
_____
_____

Year: _____ _____
_____
_____
_____

Year: _____ _____
_____
_____
_____

July 17

What do you notice first when
you look in the mirror?

Year: _____ _____

_____

_____

Year: _____ _____

_____

_____

Year: _____ _____

_____

_____

Year: _____ _____

_____

_____

Year: _____ _____

_____

_____

July 18

Were you relaxed today or stressed out?

Year: _____ _____

_____

_____

_____

Year: _____ _____

_____

_____

_____

Year: _____ _____

_____

_____

_____

Year: _____ _____

_____

_____

_____

Year: _____ _____

_____

_____

_____

July 19

Describe your day in one word.

Year: _____ _____

_____

_____

Year: _____ _____

_____

_____

Year: _____ _____

_____

_____

Year: _____ _____

_____

_____

Year: _____ _____

_____

_____

July 20

What do you wish you had
more control over?

Year: _____ _____

_____

_____

_____

Year: _____ _____

_____

_____

_____

Year: _____ _____

_____

_____

_____

Year: _____ _____

_____

_____

_____

Year: _____ _____

_____

_____

_____

July 21

What do you predict will happen before the week is over?

Year: _____

_____

_____

_____

Year: _____

_____

_____

_____

Year: _____

_____

_____

_____

Year: _____

_____

_____

_____

Year: _____

_____

_____

_____

July 22

What did you overhear today?

Year: _____ _____

_____

_____

_____

Year: _____ _____

_____

_____

_____

Year: _____ _____

_____

_____

_____

Year: _____ _____

_____

_____

_____

Year: _____ _____

_____

_____

_____

July 23

What do you wish someone would
say to you today and every day?

Year: _____

_____

_____

_____

Year: _____

_____

_____

_____

Year: _____

_____

_____

_____

Year: _____

_____

_____

_____

Year: _____

_____

_____

_____

July 24

How satisfying was your day?

Year: _____ _____

_____

_____

_____

Year: _____ _____

_____

_____

_____

Year: _____ _____

_____

_____

_____

Year: _____ _____

_____

_____

_____

Year: _____ _____

_____

_____

_____

July 25

What was the most awkward
thing that happened today?

Year: _____ _____

_____

_____

_____

Year: _____ _____

_____

_____

_____

Year: _____ _____

_____

_____

_____

Year: _____ _____

_____

_____

_____

Year: _____ _____

_____

_____

_____

July 26

What was the theme of your day?

Year: _____ _____

_____

_____

_____

Year: _____ _____

_____

_____

_____

Year: _____ _____

_____

_____

_____

Year: _____ _____

_____

_____

_____

Year: _____ _____

_____

_____

_____

July 27

What are you sensitive about right now?

Year: _____ _____

_____

_____

Year: _____ _____

_____

_____

Year: _____ _____

_____

_____

Year: _____ _____

_____

_____

Year: _____ _____

_____

_____

July 28

What is your favorite quote or saying?

Year: _____ _____

_____

_____

_____

Year: _____ _____

_____

_____

_____

Year: _____ _____

_____

_____

_____

Year: _____ _____

_____

_____

_____

Year: _____ _____

_____

_____

_____

July 29

What are you nostalgic about?

Year: _____ _____

_____

_____

_____

Year: _____ _____

_____

_____

_____

Year: _____ _____

_____

_____

_____

Year: _____ _____

_____

_____

_____

Year: _____ _____

_____

_____

_____

July 30

Would you want to live forever?

Year: _____ _____

Year: _____ _____

Year: _____ _____

Year: _____ _____

Year: _____ _____

July 31

What's the juiciest piece
of gossip you have?

Year: _____ _____

_____

_____

Year: _____ _____

_____

_____

Year: _____ _____

_____

_____

Year: _____ _____

_____

_____

Year: _____ _____

_____

_____

August 1

Do you long for solitude
or companionship?

Year: _____ _____

_____

_____

Year: _____ _____

_____

_____

_____

Year: _____ _____

_____

_____

_____

Year: _____ _____

_____

_____

_____

Year: _____ _____

_____

_____

_____

August 2

What would you put in a time capsule?

Year: _____ _____

_____

_____

Year: _____ _____

_____

_____

Year: _____ _____

_____

_____

Year: _____ _____

_____

_____

Year: _____ _____

_____

_____

August 3

What was the last thing you bragged
about (or wanted to brag about)?

Year: _____

Year: _____

Year: _____

Year: _____

Year: _____

August 4

What gets you through a tough day?

Year: _____ _____

_____

_____

Year: _____ _____

_____

_____

Year: _____ _____

_____

_____

Year: _____ _____

_____

_____

Year: _____ _____

_____

_____

August 5

Whom would you hire to play "you"
in a movie about your life?

Year: _____ _____

_____

_____

_____

Year: _____ _____

_____

_____

_____

Year: _____ _____

_____

_____

_____

Year: _____ _____

_____

_____

_____

Year: _____ _____

_____

_____

_____

August 6

What are your thoughts and
feelings about marriage?

Year: _____

Year: _____

Year: _____

Year: _____

Year: _____

August 7

What period of history
fascinates you most?

Year: _____ _____

_____

_____

Year: _____ _____

_____

_____

Year: _____ _____

_____

_____

Year: _____ _____

_____

_____

Year: _____ _____

_____

_____

August 8

_____ never fails to amaze me.

Year: _____ _____

_____

_____

_____

Year: _____ _____

_____

_____

_____

Year: _____ _____

_____

_____

_____

Year: _____ _____

_____

_____

_____

Year: _____ _____

_____

_____

_____

August 9

What side of you do few people see?

Year: _____ _____

_____

_____

_____

Year: _____ _____

_____

_____

_____

Year: _____ _____

_____

_____

_____

Year: _____ _____

_____

_____

_____

Year: _____ _____

_____

_____

_____

August 10

What would you rather not know?

Year: _____ _____

_____

_____

Year: _____ _____

_____

_____

Year: _____ _____

_____

_____

Year: _____ _____

_____

_____

Year: _____ _____

_____

_____

August 11

What do you like about the
area where you live?

Year: _____ _____

_____

_____

_____

Year: _____ _____

_____

_____

_____

Year: _____ _____

_____

_____

_____

Year: _____ _____

_____

_____

_____

Year: _____ _____

_____

_____

_____

August 12

How many true friends do you have?

Year: _____ _____

_____

_____

Year: _____ _____

_____

_____

Year: _____ _____

_____

_____

Year: _____ _____

_____

_____

Year: _____ _____

_____

_____

August 13

What was the highlight of your day?

Year: _____ _____

_____

_____

Year: _____ _____

_____

_____

Year: _____ _____

_____

_____

Year: _____ _____

_____

_____

Year: _____ _____

_____

_____

August 14

Are you having a good or bad hair day?

Year: _____ _____

_____

_____

Year: _____ _____

_____

_____

Year: _____ _____

_____

_____

Year: _____ _____

_____

_____

Year: _____ _____

_____

_____

August 15

Where do you do your best thinking?

Year: _____ _____

_____

_____

Year: _____ _____

_____

_____

Year: _____ _____

_____

_____

Year: _____ _____

_____

_____

Year: _____ _____

_____

_____

August 16

What is the oldest thing in your home?

Year: _____ _____

_____

_____

Year: _____ _____

_____

_____

Year: _____ _____

_____

_____

Year: _____ _____

_____

_____

Year: _____ _____

_____

_____

August 17

What would you like to confess?

Year: _____ _____

_____

_____

Year: _____ _____

_____

_____

Year: _____ _____

_____

_____

Year: _____ _____

_____

_____

Year: _____ _____

_____

_____

August 18

How healthy do you feel today?

Year: _____ _____

_____

_____

Year: _____ _____

_____

_____

Year: _____ _____

_____

_____

Year: _____ _____

_____

_____

Year: _____ _____

_____

_____

August 19

What do you hate throwing away?

Year: _____ _____

_____

_____

Year: _____ _____

_____

_____

Year: _____ _____

_____

_____

Year: _____ _____

_____

_____

Year: _____ _____

_____

_____

August 20

What high school or college class
has proven most useful?

Year: _____ _____

_____

_____

Year: _____ _____

_____

_____

Year: _____ _____

_____

_____

Year: _____ _____

_____

_____

Year: _____ _____

_____

_____

August 21

What's the best remedy for a bad day?

Year: _____ _____

_____

_____

_____

Year: _____ _____

_____

_____

_____

Year: _____ _____

_____

_____

_____

Year: _____ _____

_____

_____

_____

Year: _____ _____

_____

_____

_____

August 22

Who had your back today?

Year: _____ _____

_____

_____

Year: _____ _____

_____

_____

_____

Year: _____ _____

_____

_____

_____

Year: _____ _____

_____

_____

_____

Year: _____ _____

_____

_____

_____

August 23

What new person did you meet recently?

Year: _____ _____

_____

_____

_____

Year: _____ _____

_____

_____

_____

Year: _____ _____

_____

_____

_____

Year: _____ _____

_____

_____

_____

Year: _____ _____

_____

_____

_____

August 24

Who are you surprised is still your friend?

Year: _____ _____

_____

_____

_____

Year: _____ _____

_____

_____

_____

Year: _____ _____

_____

_____

_____

Year: _____ _____

_____

_____

_____

Year: _____ _____

_____

_____

_____

August 25

What story do you like to tell?

Year: _____ _____

_____

_____

Year: _____ _____

_____

_____

Year: _____ _____

_____

_____

Year: _____ _____

_____

_____

Year: _____ _____

_____

_____

August 26

_____ is the
last thing I want to do today.

Year: _____ _____

_____

_____

Year: _____ _____

_____

_____

Year: _____ _____

_____

_____

Year: _____ _____

_____

_____

Year: _____ _____

_____

_____

August 27

What is your usual breakfast?

Year: _____ _____

_____

_____

Year: _____ _____

_____

_____

Year: _____ _____

_____

_____

Year: _____ _____

_____

_____

Year: _____ _____

_____

_____

August 28

With whom do you often disagree?

Year: _____ _____

_____

_____

Year: _____ _____

_____

_____

Year: _____ _____

_____

_____

Year: _____ _____

_____

_____

Year: _____ _____

_____

_____

August 29

Is your life more of an action movie,
a drama, a thriller, or a comedy?

Year: _____ _____

_____

_____

_____

Year: _____ _____

_____

_____

_____

Year: _____ _____

_____

_____

_____

Year: _____ _____

_____

_____

_____

Year: _____ _____

_____

_____

_____

August 30

How independent are you?

Year: _____ _____

_____

_____

Year: _____ _____

_____

_____

Year: _____ _____

_____

_____

Year: _____ _____

_____

_____

Year: _____ _____

_____

_____

August 31

What is one thing you are obsessed with?

Year: _____ _____

_____

_____

Year: _____ _____

_____

_____

Year: _____ _____

_____

_____

Year: _____ _____

_____

_____

Year: _____ _____

_____

_____

September 1

Who thinks of you as a leader?

Year: _____ _____

_____

_____

_____

Year: _____ _____

_____

_____

_____

Year: _____ _____

_____

_____

_____

Year: _____ _____

_____

_____

_____

Year: _____ _____

_____

_____

_____

September 2

What is your perfect pet?

Year: _____ _____

_____

_____

Year: _____ _____

_____

_____

Year: _____ _____

_____

_____

Year: _____ _____

_____

_____

Year: _____ _____

_____

_____

September 3

_____ is heaven on Earth.

Year: _____ _____

_____

_____

Year: _____ _____

_____

_____

_____

Year: _____ _____

_____

_____

_____

Year: _____ _____

_____

_____

_____

Year: _____ _____

_____

_____

_____

September 4

What dangerous thing have
you done lately?

Year: _____ _____

_____

_____

Year: _____ _____

_____

_____

Year: _____ _____

_____

_____

Year: _____ _____

_____

_____

Year: _____ _____

_____

_____

September 5

Where did you go today?

Year: _____ _____

_____

_____

Year: _____ _____

_____

_____

Year: _____ _____

_____

_____

Year: _____ _____

_____

_____

Year: _____ _____

_____

_____

September 6

Whom would you want to be stranded
with on a deserted island?

Year: _____ _____

_____

_____

Year: _____ _____

_____

_____

Year: _____ _____

_____

_____

Year: _____ _____

_____

_____

Year: _____ _____

_____

_____

September 7

What thoughts are you distracted by today?

Year: _____ _____

_____

_____

_____

Year: _____ _____

_____

_____

_____

Year: _____ _____

_____

_____

_____

Year: _____ _____

_____

_____

_____

Year: _____ _____

_____

_____

_____

September 8

What is your beverage of choice?

Year: _____ _____

_____

_____

Year: _____ _____

_____

_____

Year: _____ _____

_____

_____

Year: _____ _____

_____

_____

Year: _____ _____

_____

_____

September 9

What did you succeed in doing today?

Year: _____

_____

_____

_____

Year: _____

_____

_____

_____

Year: _____

_____

_____

_____

Year: _____

_____

_____

_____

Year: _____

_____

_____

_____

September 10

What do you do when you can't sleep?

Year: _____ _____

_____

_____

_____

Year: _____ _____

_____

_____

_____

Year: _____ _____

_____

_____

_____

Year: _____ _____

_____

_____

_____

Year: _____ _____

_____

_____

_____

September 11

Whom would you like to honor today?

Year: _____ _____

_____

_____

_____

Year: _____ _____

_____

_____

_____

Year: _____ _____

_____

_____

_____

Year: _____ _____

_____

_____

_____

Year: _____ _____

_____

_____

_____

September 12

What issue do you tend to rant about?

Year: _____ _____
_____
_____
_____

Year: _____ _____
_____
_____
_____

Year: _____ _____
_____
_____
_____

Year: _____ _____
_____
_____
_____

Year: _____ _____
_____
_____

September 13

What is the last thing you mailed?

Year: _____

_____

_____

_____

Year: _____

_____

_____

_____

Year: _____

_____

_____

_____

Year: _____

_____

_____

_____

Year: _____

_____

_____

_____

September 14

What pet peeves do you have?

Year: _____ _____

_____

_____

_____

Year: _____ _____

_____

_____

_____

Year: _____ _____

_____

_____

_____

Year: _____ _____

_____

_____

_____

Year: _____ _____

_____

_____

_____

September 15

Whom would you call in an emergency?

Year: _____ _____

_____

_____

Year: _____ _____

_____

_____

Year: _____ _____

_____

_____

Year: _____ _____

_____

_____

Year: _____ _____

_____

_____

September 16

How fun are you at parties?

Year: _____ _____

_____

_____

_____

Year: _____ _____

_____

_____

_____

Year: _____ _____

_____

_____

_____

Year: _____ _____

_____

_____

_____

Year: _____ _____

_____

_____

_____

September 17

What is the last thing you got for free?

Year: _____ _____

_____

_____

Year: _____ _____

_____

_____

Year: _____ _____

_____

_____

Year: _____ _____

_____

_____

Year: _____ _____

_____

_____

September 18

What do you look forward
to about tomorrow?

Year: _____ _____

_____

_____

_____

Year: _____ _____

_____

_____

_____

Year: _____ _____

_____

_____

_____

Year: _____ _____

_____

_____

_____

Year: _____ _____

_____

_____

_____

September 19

What plan are you devising?

Year: _____ _____

_____

_____

_____

Year: _____ _____

_____

_____

_____

Year: _____ _____

_____

_____

_____

Year: _____ _____

_____

_____

_____

Year: _____ _____

_____

_____

_____

September 20

Who needs you more than you need them?

Year: _____ _____

_____

_____

Year: _____ _____

_____

_____

Year: _____ _____

_____

_____

Year: _____ _____

_____

_____

Year: _____ _____

_____

_____

September 21

What do people lecture you about?

Year: _____ _____

_____

_____

Year: _____ _____

_____

_____

Year: _____ _____

_____

_____

Year: _____ _____

_____

_____

Year: _____ _____

_____

_____

September 22

Who bores you to tears?

Year: _____ _____

_____

_____

_____

Year: _____ _____

_____

_____

_____

Year: _____ _____

_____

_____

_____

Year: _____ _____

_____

_____

_____

Year: _____ _____

_____

_____

_____

September 23

Where do you feel at home: oceans,
mountains, or wide-open plains?

Year: _____ _____

_____

_____

_____

Year: _____ _____

_____

_____

_____

Year: _____ _____

_____

_____

_____

Year: _____ _____

_____

_____

_____

Year: _____ _____

_____

_____

_____

September 24

My biggest adventure was
when I _____.

Year: _____

Year: _____

Year: _____

Year: _____

Year: _____

September 25

Don't talk to me when I'm _____.

Year: _____ _____

_____

_____

Year: _____ _____

_____

_____

Year: _____ _____

_____

_____

Year: _____ _____

_____

_____

Year: _____ _____

_____

_____

September 26

How well did you treat the environment today?

Year: _____ _____

_____

_____

Year: _____ _____

_____

_____

Year: _____ _____

_____

_____

Year: _____ _____

_____

_____

Year: _____ _____

_____

_____

September 27

What colors do you wear most often?

Year: _____ _____

_____

_____

Year: _____ _____

_____

_____

_____

Year: _____ _____

_____

_____

_____

Year: _____ _____

_____

_____

_____

Year: _____ _____

_____

_____

_____

September 28

When did you last trust your instincts?

Year: _____ _____

_____

_____

Year: _____ _____

_____

_____

Year: _____ _____

_____

_____

Year: _____ _____

_____

_____

Year: _____ _____

_____

_____

September 29

What guilty pleasures do you enjoy?

Year: _____ _____

_____

_____

Year: _____ _____

_____

_____

Year: _____ _____

_____

_____

Year: _____ _____

_____

_____

Year: _____ _____

_____

_____

September 30

What do you value most in life?

Year: _____ _____

_____

_____

_____

Year: _____ _____

_____

_____

_____

Year: _____ _____

_____

_____

_____

Year: _____ _____

_____

_____

_____

Year: _____ _____

_____

_____

_____

October 1

What experience changed you?

Year: _____ _____

_____

_____

Year: _____ _____

_____

_____

Year: _____ _____

_____

_____

Year: _____ _____

_____

_____

Year: _____ _____

_____

_____

October 2

Make a wish.

Year: _____ _____

_____

_____

Year: _____ _____

_____

_____

Year: _____ _____

_____

_____

Year: _____ _____

_____

_____

Year: _____ _____

_____

_____

October 3

What advice would you like to share?

Year: _____ _____

_____

_____

Year: _____ _____

_____

_____

Year: _____ _____

_____

_____

Year: _____ _____

_____

_____

Year: _____ _____

_____

_____

October 4

What blows your mind?

Year: _____ _____

_____

_____

Year: _____ _____

_____

_____

Year: _____ _____

_____

_____

Year: _____ _____

_____

_____

Year: _____ _____

_____

_____

October 5

What can you never get enough of?

Year: _____ _____

_____

_____

Year: _____ _____

_____

_____

Year: _____ _____

_____

_____

Year: _____ _____

_____

_____

Year: _____ _____

_____

_____

October 6

With whom would you like to switch bodies?

Year: _____ _____

_____

_____

_____

Year: _____ _____

_____

_____

_____

Year: _____ _____

_____

_____

_____

Year: _____ _____

_____

_____

_____

Year: _____ _____

_____

_____

_____

October 7

Whose mind do you wish you could read?

Year: _____ _____

_____

_____

_____

Year: _____ _____

_____

_____

_____

Year: _____ _____

_____

_____

_____

Year: _____ _____

_____

_____

_____

Year: _____ _____

_____

_____

_____

October 8

What part of today would
you like to relive in slow motion?

Year: _____ _____

_____

_____

_____

Year: _____ _____

_____

_____

_____

Year: _____ _____

_____

_____

_____

Year: _____ _____

_____

_____

_____

Year: _____ _____

_____

_____

_____

October 9

When are you most productive?

Year: _____ _____

_____

_____

_____

Year: _____ _____

_____

_____

_____

Year: _____ _____

_____

_____

_____

Year: _____ _____

_____

_____

_____

Year: _____ _____

_____

_____

_____

October 10

*What do you tend to do
when you're nervous?*

Year: _____   _____

_____

_____

_____

Year: _____   _____

_____

_____

_____

Year: _____   _____

_____

_____

_____

Year: _____   _____

_____

_____

_____

Year: _____   _____

_____

_____

_____

October 11

What fears are you facing?

Year: _____ _____

_____

_____

_____

Year: _____ _____

_____

_____

_____

Year: _____ _____

_____

_____

_____

Year: _____ _____

_____

_____

_____

Year: _____ _____

_____

_____

_____

October 12

Who would you bring back from
the dead if you could?

Year: _____ _____

_____

_____

Year: _____ _____

_____

_____

Year: _____ _____

_____

_____

Year: _____ _____

_____

_____

Year: _____ _____

_____

_____

October 13

What is the last thing you saw
or heard that moved you?

Year: _____ _____

_____

_____

_____

Year: _____ _____

_____

_____

_____

Year: _____ _____

_____

_____

_____

Year: _____ _____

_____

_____

_____

Year: _____ _____

_____

_____

_____

October 14

What instrument do you
wish you could play?

Year: _____ _____

_____

_____

Year: _____ _____

_____

_____

Year: _____ _____

_____

_____

Year: _____ _____

_____

_____

Year: _____ _____

_____

_____

October 15

What's the last thing you made by hand?

Year: _____ _____

_____

_____

Year: _____ _____

_____

_____

Year: _____ _____

_____

_____

Year: _____ _____

_____

_____

Year: _____ _____

_____

_____

October 16

If you called in "sick," how
would you spend the day?

Year: _____ _____

_____

_____

_____

Year: _____ _____

_____

_____

_____

Year: _____ _____

_____

_____

_____

Year: _____ _____

_____

_____

_____

Year: _____ _____

_____

_____

_____

October 17

What is the best and worst
thing that happened today?

Year: _____

_____

_____

_____

Year: _____

_____

_____

_____

Year: _____

_____

_____

_____

Year: _____

_____

_____

_____

Year: _____

_____

_____

_____

October 18

What required extra patience today?

Year: _____ _____

_____

_____

Year: _____ _____

_____

_____

Year: _____ _____

_____

_____

Year: _____ _____

_____

_____

Year: _____ _____

_____

_____

October 19

What are you proud to have done today?

Year: _____ _____

_____

_____

_____

Year: _____ _____

_____

_____

_____

Year: _____ _____

_____

_____

_____

Year: _____ _____

_____

_____

_____

Year: _____ _____

_____

_____

_____

October 20

What Halloween costume
do you plan to wear?

Year: _____ _____

_____

_____

_____

Year: _____ _____

_____

_____

_____

Year: _____ _____

_____

_____

_____

Year: _____ _____

_____

_____

_____

Year: _____ _____

_____

_____

_____

October 21

How would you describe your style?

Year: _____ _____

_____

_____

_____

Year: _____ _____

_____

_____

_____

Year: _____ _____

_____

_____

_____

Year: _____ _____

_____

_____

_____

Year: _____ _____

_____

_____

_____

October 22

What was the most enjoyable
thing you ate today?

Year: _____ _____

_____

_____

Year: _____ _____

_____

_____

Year: _____ _____

_____

_____

Year: _____ _____

_____

_____

Year: _____ _____

_____

_____

October 23

Who has you wrapped around his/her finger?

Year: _____ _____

_____

_____

Year: _____ _____

_____

_____

Year: _____ _____

_____

_____

Year: _____ _____

_____

_____

Year: _____ _____

_____

_____

October 24

What is your favorite scary movie?

Year: _____ _____

_____

_____

Year: _____ _____

_____

_____

Year: _____ _____

_____

_____

Year: _____ _____

_____

_____

Year: _____ _____

_____

_____

October 25

If you could be reincarnated,
whom/what would you return as?

Year: _____

Year: _____

Year: _____

Year: _____

Year: _____

October 26

What national problem gets you fired up?

Year: _____ _____

_____

_____

Year: _____ _____

_____

_____

Year: _____ _____

_____

_____

Year: _____ _____

_____

_____

Year: _____ _____

_____

_____

October 27

Describe the most recent fight you had.

Year: _____ _____

_____

_____

_____

Year: _____ _____

_____

_____

_____

Year: _____ _____

_____

_____

_____

Year: _____ _____

_____

_____

_____

Year: _____ _____

_____

_____

_____

October 28

What does your award acceptance
speech sound like?

Year: _____ _____

_____

_____

_____

Year: _____ _____

_____

_____

_____

Year: _____ _____

_____

_____

_____

Year: _____ _____

_____

_____

_____

Year: _____ _____

_____

_____

_____

October 29

Highway or back roads?

Year: _____ _____

_____

_____

_____

Year: _____ _____

_____

_____

_____

Year: _____ _____

_____

_____

_____

Year: _____ _____

_____

_____

_____

Year: _____ _____

_____

_____

_____

October 30

What is the last thing you won?

Year: _____ _____

_____

_____

_____

Year: _____ _____

_____

_____

_____

Year: _____ _____

_____

_____

_____

Year: _____ _____

_____

_____

_____

Year: _____ _____

_____

_____

_____

October 31

What scares you the most?

Year: _____ _____

_____

_____

Year: _____ _____

_____

_____

Year: _____ _____

_____

_____

Year: _____ _____

_____

_____

Year: _____ _____

_____

_____

November 1

At what age do you plan to retire?

Year: _____ _____

_____

_____

_____

Year: _____ _____

_____

_____

_____

Year: _____ _____

_____

_____

_____

Year: _____ _____

_____

_____

_____

Year: _____ _____

_____

_____

_____

November 2

What wild animal would you like
to keep as a pet if you could?

Year: _____ _____

_____

_____

_____

Year: _____ _____

_____

_____

_____

Year: _____ _____

_____

_____

_____

Year: _____ _____

_____

_____

_____

Year: _____ _____

_____

_____

_____

November 3

What plans have you put on hold?

Year: _____ _____

_____

_____

_____

Year: _____ _____

_____

_____

_____

Year: _____ _____

_____

_____

_____

Year: _____ _____

_____

_____

_____

Year: _____ _____

_____

_____

_____

November 4

Who is the last person you hugged?

Year: _____ _____

_____

_____

Year: _____ _____

_____

_____

Year: _____ _____

_____

_____

Year: _____ _____

_____

_____

Year: _____ _____

_____

_____

November 5

What song would you choose if
you were in a karaoke contest?

Year: _____ _____

_____

_____

_____

Year: _____ _____

_____

_____

_____

Year: _____ _____

_____

_____

_____

Year: _____ _____

_____

_____

_____

Year: _____ _____

_____

_____

_____

November 6

What made you stop and think today?

Year: _____ _____

_____

_____

Year: _____ _____

_____

_____

Year: _____ _____

_____

_____

Year: _____ _____

_____

_____

Year: _____ _____

_____

_____

November 7

What is the best thing about you?

Year: _____ _____

_____

_____

Year: _____ _____

_____

_____

Year: _____ _____

_____

_____

Year: _____ _____

_____

_____

_____

Year: _____ _____

_____

_____

November 8

How do you like to celebrate
your birthday?

Year: _____

_____

_____

_____

Year: _____

_____

_____

_____

Year: _____

_____

_____

_____

Year: _____

_____

_____

_____

Year: _____

_____

_____

_____

November 9

What day would you like to
relive if you could?

Year: _____ _____

_____

_____

_____

Year: _____ _____

_____

_____

_____

Year: _____ _____

_____

_____

_____

Year: _____ _____

_____

_____

_____

Year: _____ _____

_____

_____

_____

November 10

At what point will you know you've made it?

Year: _____ _____

_____

_____

_____

Year: _____ _____

_____

_____

_____

Year: _____ _____

_____

_____

_____

Year: _____ _____

_____

_____

_____

Year: _____ _____

_____

_____

_____

November 11

What celebrity do you most resemble?

Year: _____ _____

_____

_____

_____

Year: _____ _____

_____

_____

_____

Year: _____ _____

_____

_____

_____

Year: _____ _____

_____

_____

_____

Year: _____ _____

_____

_____

_____

November 12

Who is your idol?

Year: _____ _____

_____

_____

_____

Year: _____ _____

_____

_____

_____

Year: _____ _____

_____

_____

_____

Year: _____ _____

_____

_____

_____

Year: _____ _____

_____

_____

_____

November 13

What do you wish you could
tell your younger self?

Year: _____ _____

_____

_____

_____

Year: _____ _____

_____

_____

_____

Year: _____ _____

_____

_____

_____

Year: _____ _____

_____

_____

_____

Year: _____ _____

_____

_____

_____

November 14

_____ is completely overrated.

Year: _____ _____

_____

_____

Year: _____ _____

_____

_____

Year: _____ _____

_____

_____

Year: _____ _____

_____

_____

Year: _____ _____

_____

_____

November 15

_____ is completely underrated.

Year: _____   _____

_____

_____

Year: _____   _____

_____

_____

Year: _____   _____

_____

_____

Year: _____   _____

_____

_____

Year: _____   _____

_____

_____

November 16

What is the last book you recommended?

Year: _____

Year: _____

Year: _____

Year: _____

Year: _____

November 17

What words do you love the sound of?

Year: _____ _____

_____

_____

Year: _____ _____

_____

_____

Year: _____ _____

_____

_____

Year: _____ _____

_____

_____

Year: _____ _____

_____

_____

November 18

There's no end to my love
for _____.

Year: _____

Year: _____

Year: _____

Year: _____

Year: _____

November 19

I'm a wimp when it comes to _____.

Year: _____

_____

_____

_____

Year: _____

_____

_____

_____

Year: _____

_____

_____

_____

Year: _____

_____

_____

_____

Year: _____

_____

_____

_____

November 20

Being around children makes
me _____.

Year: _____

_____

_____

_____

Year: _____

_____

_____

_____

Year: _____

_____

_____

_____

Year: _____

_____

_____

_____

Year: _____

_____

_____

_____

November 21

What do you have a hard time believing?

Year: _____ _____

_____

_____

_____

Year: _____ _____

_____

_____

_____

Year: _____ _____

_____

_____

_____

Year: _____ _____

_____

_____

_____

Year: _____ _____

_____

_____

_____

November 22

What wisdom has been shared with you?

Year: _____

_____

_____

_____

Year: _____

_____

_____

_____

Year: _____

_____

_____

_____

Year: _____

_____

_____

_____

Year: _____

_____

_____

_____

November 23

What did you daydream about today?

Year: _____

_____

_____

_____

Year: _____

_____

_____

_____

Year: _____

_____

_____

_____

Year: _____

_____

_____

_____

Year: _____

_____

_____

_____

November 24

What were you born to do?

Year: _____ _____

_____

_____

Year: _____ _____

_____

_____

Year: _____ _____

_____

_____

Year: _____ _____

_____

_____

Year: _____ _____

_____

_____

November 25

What do you need to go shopping for?

Year: _____ _____

_____

_____

_____

Year: _____ _____

_____

_____

_____

Year: _____ _____

_____

_____

_____

Year: _____ _____

_____

_____

_____

Year: _____ _____

_____

_____

_____

November 26

Who fascinates you?

Year: _____ _____

_____

_____

_____

Year: _____ _____

_____

_____

_____

Year: _____ _____

_____

_____

_____

Year: _____ _____

_____

_____

_____

Year: _____ _____

_____

_____

_____

November 27

What are you most thankful for today?

Year: _____ _____

_____

_____

_____

Year: _____ _____

_____

_____

_____

Year: _____ _____

_____

_____

_____

Year: _____ _____

_____

_____

_____

Year: _____ _____

_____

_____

_____

November 28

When was the last time you were in big trouble?

Year: _____ _____

_____

_____

Year: _____ _____

_____

_____

Year: _____ _____

_____

_____

Year: _____ _____

_____

_____

Year: _____ _____

_____

_____

November 29

What emoji do you use the most?

Year: _____ _____

_____

_____

_____

Year: _____ _____

_____

_____

_____

Year: _____ _____

_____

_____

_____

Year: _____ _____

_____

_____

_____

Year: _____ _____

_____

_____

_____

November 30

What are you searching for?

Year: _____ _____

_____

_____

Year: _____ _____

_____

_____

Year: _____ _____

_____

_____

Year: _____ _____

_____

_____

Year: _____ _____

_____

_____

December 1

What comes up when you
Google your name?

Year: _____ _____

_____

_____

Year: _____ _____

_____

_____

Year: _____ _____

_____

_____

Year: _____ _____

_____

_____

Year: _____ _____

_____

_____

December 2

Where do you go for answers?

Year: _____ _____

_____

_____

_____

Year: _____ _____

_____

_____

_____

Year: _____ _____

_____

_____

_____

Year: _____ _____

_____

_____

_____

Year: _____ _____

_____

_____

_____

December 3

Who would you make a toast to
today? What would you say?

Year: _____ _____
_____
_____
_____

Year: _____ _____
_____
_____
_____

Year: _____ _____
_____
_____
_____

Year: _____ _____
_____
_____
_____

Year: _____ _____
_____
_____
_____

December 4

What made you panic recently?

Year: _____

Year: _____

Year: _____

Year: _____

Year: _____

December 5

What food do you avoid at all cost?

Year: _____

Year: _____

Year: _____

Year: _____

Year: _____

December 6

When is the last time you were
outside your comfort zone?

Year: _____ _____

_____

_____

Year: _____ _____

_____

_____

Year: _____ _____

_____

_____

Year: _____ _____

_____

_____

Year: _____ _____

_____

_____

December 7

When did you feel your best today?

Year: _____ _____

_____

_____

_____

Year: _____ _____

_____

_____

_____

Year: _____ _____

_____

_____

_____

Year: _____ _____

_____

_____

_____

Year: _____ _____

_____

_____

_____

December 8

Do you live mostly in the past,
the present, or the future?

Year: _____ _____

_____

_____

_____

Year: _____ _____

_____

_____

_____

Year: _____ _____

_____

_____

_____

Year: _____ _____

_____

_____

_____

Year: _____ _____

_____

_____

_____

December 9

How confident do you feel today?

Year: _____ _____

_____

_____

_____

Year: _____ _____

_____

_____

_____

Year: _____ _____

_____

_____

_____

Year: _____ _____

_____

_____

_____

Year: _____ _____

_____

_____

_____

December 10

How would you describe the
state of the world?

Year: _____

_____

_____

Year: _____

_____

_____

Year: _____

_____

_____

Year: _____

_____

_____

Year: _____

_____

_____

December 11

What challenge are you facing?

Year: _____ _____

_____

_____

Year: _____ _____

_____

_____

Year: _____ _____

_____

_____

Year: _____ _____

_____

_____

Year: _____ _____

_____

_____

December 12

What do you need most today?

Year: _____ _____

_____

_____

Year: _____ _____

_____

_____

Year: _____ _____

_____

_____

Year: _____ _____

_____

_____

Year: _____ _____

_____

_____

December 13

Paper, plastic, or reusable?

Year: _____ _____

_____

_____

_____

Year: _____ _____

_____

_____

_____

Year: _____ _____

_____

_____

_____

Year: _____ _____

_____

_____

_____

Year: _____ _____

_____

_____

_____

December 14

What is your favorite building?

Year: _____ _____

_____

_____

Year: _____ _____

_____

_____

Year: _____ _____

_____

_____

Year: _____ _____

_____

_____

Year: _____ _____

_____

_____

December 15

Do plants thrive or die in your care?

Year: _____ _____

_____

_____

Year: _____ _____

_____

_____

Year: _____ _____

_____

_____

Year: _____ _____

_____

_____

_____

Year: _____ _____

_____

_____

_____

December 16

What rule do you often break?

Year: _____

Year: _____

Year: _____

Year: _____

Year: _____

December 17

The true measure of a man or
woman is _____.

Year: _____   _____

_____

_____

_____

Year: _____   _____

_____

_____

_____

Year: _____   _____

_____

_____

_____

Year: _____   _____

_____

_____

_____

Year: _____   _____

_____

_____

_____

December 18

One item on my bucket list
is _____.

Year: _____   _____
_____
_____
_____

Year: _____   _____
_____
_____
_____

Year: _____   _____
_____
_____
_____

Year: _____   _____
_____
_____
_____

Year: _____   _____
_____
_____
_____

December 19

What makes you feel safe?

Year: _____ _____

_____

_____

_____

Year: _____ _____

_____

_____

_____

Year: _____ _____

_____

_____

_____

Year: _____ _____

_____

_____

_____

Year: _____ _____

_____

_____

_____

December 20

What is the last thing you shared?

Year: _____ _____

_____

_____

_____

Year: _____ _____

_____

_____

_____

Year: _____ _____

_____

_____

_____

Year: _____ _____

_____

_____

_____

Year: _____ _____

_____

_____

December 21

Who thinks you are funny?

Year: _____ _____

_____

_____

_____

Year: _____ _____

_____

_____

_____

Year: _____ _____

_____

_____

_____

Year: _____ _____

_____

_____

_____

Year: _____ _____

_____

_____

_____

December 22

What is the last thing you quit?

Year: _____ _____

Year: _____ _____

Year: _____ _____

Year: _____ _____

Year: _____ _____

December 23

What is the weirdest thing about you?

Year: _____ _____

_____

_____

_____

Year: _____ _____

_____

_____

_____

Year: _____ _____

_____

_____

_____

Year: _____ _____

_____

_____

_____

Year: _____ _____

_____

_____

_____

December 24

Is your life currently a
smooth ride or an off-road adventure?

Year: _____ _____

_____

_____

_____

Year: _____ _____

_____

_____

_____

Year: _____ _____

_____

_____

_____

Year: _____ _____

_____

_____

_____

Year: _____ _____

_____

_____

_____

December 25

What is the best gift you've received?

Year: _____ _____
_____
_____
_____

Year: _____ _____
_____
_____
_____

Year: _____ _____
_____
_____
_____

Year: _____ _____
_____
_____
_____

Year: _____ _____
_____
_____
_____

December 26

When was the last time you misjudged someone?

Year: _____ _____

_____

_____

Year: _____ _____

_____

_____

Year: _____ _____

_____

_____

Year: _____ _____

_____

_____

Year: _____ _____

_____

_____

December 27

What have you been holding in?

Year: _____ _____
_____
_____
_____

Year: _____ _____
_____
_____
_____

Year: _____ _____
_____
_____
_____

Year: _____ _____
_____
_____
_____

Year: _____ _____
_____
_____
_____

December 28

What recurring dream do you have?

Year: _____ _____

_____

_____

_____

Year: _____ _____

_____

_____

_____

Year: _____ _____

_____

_____

_____

Year: _____ _____

_____

_____

_____

Year: _____ _____

_____

_____

_____

December 29

What do you hope for?

Year: _____ _____

_____

_____

_____

Year: _____ _____

_____

_____

_____

Year: _____ _____

_____

_____

_____

Year: _____ _____

_____

_____

_____

Year: _____ _____

_____

_____

_____

December 30

How much do you enjoy
writing in this journal?

Year: _____ _____

_____

_____

Year: _____ _____

_____

_____

Year: _____ _____

_____

_____

Year: _____ _____

_____

_____

Year: _____ _____

_____

_____

December 31

What is your favorite memory
from this year?

Year: _____ _____

_____

_____

Year: _____ _____

_____

_____

Year: _____ _____

_____

_____

Year: _____ _____

_____

_____

Year: _____ _____

_____

_____